Math My Activity Book

(Addition, Subtraction and Shapes)

Wonder Dough Learning Through Art

Rohana Amran

ISBN
978-1-5437-4745-4 (sc)
978-1-5437-4746-1 (e)

Print information available on the last page.

To order additional copies of this book, contact
Toll Free 800 101 2657 (Singapore)
Toll Free 1 800 81 7340 (Malaysia)
www.partridgepublishing.com/singapore
orders.singapore@partridgepublishing.com

08/25/2018

PARTRIDGE

Notes to parents and educators.

Use Wonder Dough to create numbers, shapes and objects that you and your child like.
For more information on how to use this book, visit our FaceBook page:

https://www.facebook.com/wonderdoughbywunderkind/

To order Wonder Dough

please contact through WhatsApp +65 97895162

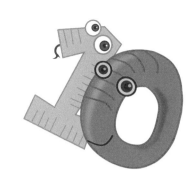

Counting

one

two

three

four

five

six

seven

eight

seven

eight

nine

ten

Shapes

Circle

square

oval

pentagon

hexagon

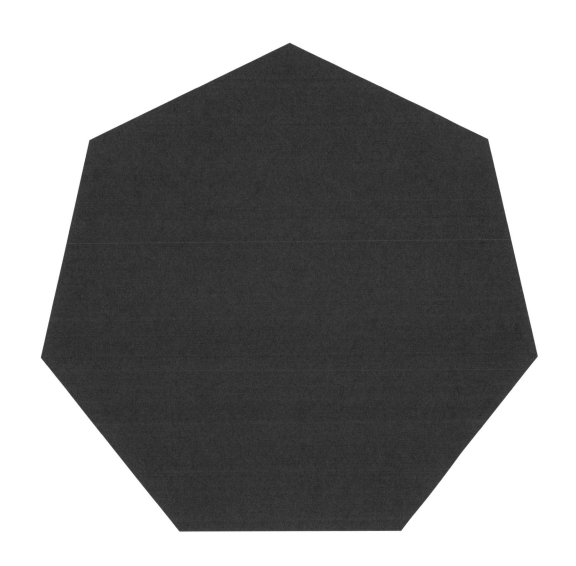

heptagon

octagon

heart

Addition

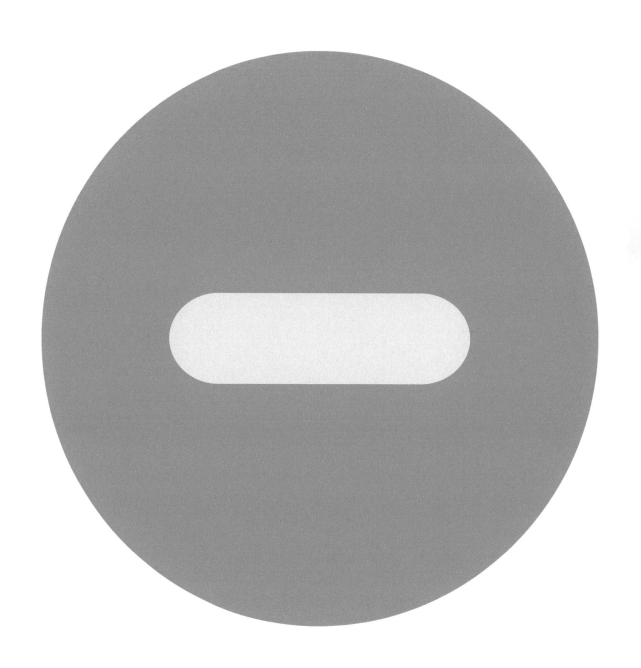

Subtraction

5 - 3 =

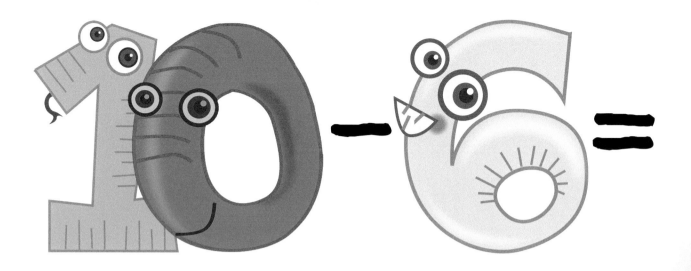

10 - 6 =

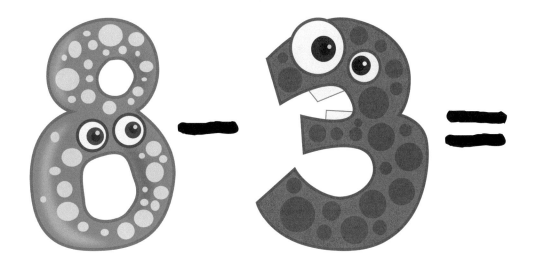

10 - 4 =

Create your own addition

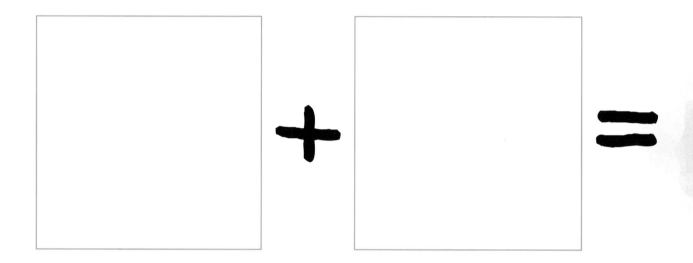

Create your own subtraction

Printed in the United States
By Bookmasters